CANCER!
NOW
WHAT?

Copyright © 2017 by Carmem Carmo

Project Manager: Marcus Lima

Cover: Marcus Lima

Diagramming: Rovan Berto

Review: Yael Botelho

Printing and Binding: CreateSpace by Amazon

All Scripture quotations were taken from the English Standard Version (ESV).

International Cataloging Data in Publication

Carmo, Carmem, 2017.
  Cancer! Now What? / Carmem Carmo
  94p; 12x28cm.

Printed in the United States of America

Dedicated to the One that is able to heal all my diseases in my body, soul, and spirit.

Acknowlegments

I want to thank...

My husband Jefferson who was willing to take upon himself my sickness.

My oldest daughter Acsa who made a great sacrifice to stay with me in my nastiest moments.

My son Pedro who wanted to take care of and protect me and give me time to heal.

My youngest daughter Gabriela (Bia) who was there for me through the entire journey.

My family in blood and my spiritual family for your prayers and encouraging words.

To First Baptist Orlando who gave me all the support I needed to overcome both as my home church and employer.

The First Life Center for Pregnancy's staff and volunteers for loving me even in my weakest moments.

My dear friend Melanie who insisted on having me checked as soon as possible.

The Rosique family in Brazil for taking care of me.

About the author

Dr. **Carmem Carmo** was born in Brazil. She accepted Jesus as her Savior at the age of 11. When she was 15 years old, she was called to be a missionary. She attended Seminary in her hometown, Goiania, after graduating from high school. In 1989, she got married to Jefferson Carmo. They have three children: Acsa, born in 1991; Pedro, born in 1992; Gabriela 1994. In 2012 they opened their family to receive Paulo Junior as son-in-law. In 2014 they welcome their first granddaughter, Rebecah. In 2017 Isabella was born, their second grandchild.

Their family moved to the USA in 1996 as missionaries. They lived in the Boston area for

5 years and planted 5 Portuguese speaking churches in the Boston area. While in Boston, Carmem was first contacted by a Center for Pregnancy to help with a Brazilian young lady who wanted an abortion.

In 2001, they moved to Jacksonville, North Carolina where their family worked to improve their English. At that time, Carmem became the director of a Pregnancy Center. Then they moved to Orlando in 2002 and she started volunteering at the First Life Center for Pregnancy while getting her Master Degree in Christian Counseling. In 2016 she received her PhD in Clinical Christian Counseling from Florida Christian University. Today she is the director with a heart for serving our community with the love of Jesus.

Cancer! Now What?

It was a Tuesday evening. I just got home from work. My dear husband called me from the living room. I went to him and he asked me to sit down. I knew it couldn't be good.

He told me that the doctor from Brazil had called with the biopsy results. It was positive. I needed to find an oncologist here in the USA and have it removed.

I started crying. My son came downstairs and asked what was going on. I asked my husband to tell him and my youngest daughter. They all started crying.

I was crying not because I was afraid to die or afraid of not see my children graduating, getting married and having children. I was crying because I knew that cancer's journey is a hard and difficult one.

Today I'm cancer free! Today I'm a cancer survivor! I want to share with you how I got here, from victim to victorious.

"For I know the plans I have for you," declares the Lord, "plans to prosper you and not to harm you, plans to give you hope and a future" Jeremiah 29:11

The News

"They will have no fear of bad
news; their hearts are steadfast,
trusting in the Lord."
- Psalm 112:7

First thing I did after I got the news was talk
to my doctor in Brazil. I told him that whatever
the outcome, I was victorious. If God healed me
I was going to give Him the Glory. If I died, I
was going to have a new body and live without
pain in heaven with Jesus.

That was the most important thing in my recovery. My faith in my heavenly Father was and is what carries me on. I gave Jesus my sickness and trusted Him to take me to the place He wanted me to be.

When I let it go and rested in Him, I experienced amazing things. I knew the Lord heals. I have seen Him do it so many times. I knew He is the Doctor of the doctors. I knew He is powerful to take away all diseases but I experienced that in my life for the first time.

I can say Jesus is my Healer! He carried me through this hardship and I couldn't do it without His Love and care.

If you got the same results I got or know someone who has, you need to know God as the Great Healer.

"I know that you can do
all things; no purpose of yours
can be thwarted. My ears
had heard of you but now my
eyes have seen you."
- Job 42:2, 5

Where I Am Going

"Jesus answered, 'I am the way
the truth and the life. No one
comes to the Father except
through me.'"
- John 14:6

When I understood that I was a sinner and I was
separated from God, I made a decision to accept
what Jesus did for me on the cross. He paid
the price of my mistakes. I deserved eternal
separation from my Heavenly Father; but by His
Grace I don't have to be separated from Him.

That day I received something amazing: all my sins were forgiven. Not only that, I found out that Heaven is my destination. Jesus is not on the cross anymore. He's alive and in heaven preparing a place for me.

Every morning I praise the Lord for the reality that I'm one day closer to the day I'll live with Him forever.

That makes everything else that I go through in life seem so temporary.

Because I knew where I was going, it helped me in my healing journey. Not being afraid of the future gave me the strength to fight in the present.

Every time I remembered I had received the news that my test results were positive for cancer, I knew I didn't have to be afraid. The worst case scenario was me dying with this disease. And I have the promise of eternity in heaven.

I pray that you know too where you are going because it will help you to face today's challenges.

"Look! God's dwelling place is now among the people, and he will dwell with them. They will be his people, and God himself will be with them and be their God. 'He will wipe every tear from their eyes. There will be no more death' or mourning or crying or pain, for the old order of things has passed away."
- Revelation 21:3,4

I Belong

"He came to that which was
his own, but his own did not
receive him. Yet to all who
did receive him, to those who
believed in his name, he gave
the right to become children of
God."
- John 1:11-12

When I was 7 years old I lost my father from
heart disease. As a result, I grew up trying
to find where I belonged. At 11 years of age I

found God as my father. I found the love I was looking for. The amazing thing is that with that I got a new family. The Body of Christ is where I belong now.

I was surprised by all the love, care, and support I received. People around the world started sending encouraging words. I had people praying for me and fasting for my healing.

I can say for sure that helped me immensely to get where I'm today.

I have the privilege to work in a wonderful church. I received support from the leadership and all with whom I came in contact with. Throughout the whole process, I saw everyone's love and concern for me.

I was not alone. I'm never alone.

Look around you. The Lord will send people to be there for you. They will give you the support and love you need to overcome your challenges.

"And the prayer offered
in faith will make the sick
person well; the Lord will
raise them up."
- James 5:15

Next Step

"For those who are led by the
Spirit of God are the children
of God. The Spirit you received
does not make you slaves, so
that you live in fear again;
rather, the Spirit you received
brought about your adoption
to sonship. And by him we cry,
'Abba, Father.'"
- Romans 8:14-15

The next step after I got the biopsy results was to find the right doctor and treatment. When I talked to my Brazilian doctor he said to me, "Carmem please do me a favor: Do whatever the doctors advise you to do. It won't be easy but follow their direction."

I trusted in God to send me to the right doctor. I went online and the first thing that popped out on Breast Cancer was a Christian Hospital. I gave them a call and I received such an encouraging response. I hung up knowing I had someone really interested in my case and willing to help me in my journey to recovery.

It is so good to know that the Lord knew I was going to be in Orlando when I got this news. He provided the right professionals to help me in my weakness.

Ask the Father to send the right professionals to take care of you and the ones you love. Trust these professionals because they're instruments in God's hand to bring healing.

"And my God will meet all
your needs according to
the riches of his glory in
Christ Jesus."
- Philippians 4:19

5

Let It Go

"Commit your way to the Lord,
trust in him and he will do this."
- Psalm 37:5

From the moment I received the cancer diagnosis to the news that I was "Cancer Free" I had to let it go.

My mind was in a big cloud and nothing was clear. I had to talk to different doctors and make decisions about the treatment plan.

I didn't have full knowledge of my condition and the doctors needed more tests and surgeries to give me the answers I needed.

I did everything I was asked to do, but every step of the way I asked Jesus to be my Healer. I had to trust Him 100%.

I learned with my sickness that we're not in control of our lives. We can try but we fail all the time.

When I saw the oncologist for the first time I asked her, "What did I do wrong to cause this?"

I always tried to be active and eat right. I didn't drink alcohol, do drugs or smoke. I tried to keep my body as healthy as possible. But I still got sick.

Her answer was, "I'll tell you right now that you didn't do anything wrong. And try not to blame yourself or find the reason you got this. In the USA 1 woman out of 6 gets breast cancer. You are one of them."

Knowing that helped me to let go of the "Why" and to give control to the Lord.

I hope you find this place of rest. Trust Jesus 100%. Give it all to God.

"For whoever wants to
save their life will lose it,
but whoever loses their life
for me will save it."
- Luke 9:24

6

Keep Going

"As for you, go your way
till the end. You will rest,
and then at the end of the days
you will rise to receive your
allotted inheritance."
- Daniel 12:13

On the first day after I got my bad news, I had a meeting with my supervisor. When I let him know about the test results, God used him to encourage me. He assured me that I was going to have all the support I needed from the church as my employer and as Christ's body. And I got it.

I got a promotion so I could have the health insurance needed for the treatment.

The prayer ministry sent me a special handmade quilt that they prayed over so I could take it with me to my treatments.

All my co-workers got an extra load of work to help me. They could tell when I was having a bad day and would be patient with me. Because of that I was able to come to work. That helped me so much. Even when my energy level was low I pushed myself to go to work.

The Lord even opened the door for two of my co-workers and myself to go to China between two of my chemotherapies. We were able to help the Chinese people see the gift of life they receive when they're pregnant. In my weak state, the Lord still used me to blessed those sweet brothers and sisters.

Being around people kept my mind away from my own problems.

If you or someone you know is going through a similar situation encourage them to stay active and help them in their weakness.

"But he said to me, 'My grace is sufficient for you, for my power is made perfect in weakness.' Therefore I will boast all the more gladly about my weaknesses, so that Christ's power may rest on me. That is why, for Christ's sake, I delight in weaknesses, in insults, in hardships, in persecutions, in difficulties. For when I am weak, then I am strong."
- 2Corinthians 12:9-10

7

The Word

**"Jesus answered, 'It is written: 'Man shall not live on bread alone, but on every word that comes from the mouth of God.'"
- Matthew 4:4**

During the treatments, my head wasn't completely clear. I felt like there was a cloud around my mind. Not much was sticking to it. My memory wasn't working very well but I was able to remember some of God's promises to me. I kept them in front of me to help me to keep my eyes on what is eternal and not on what is temporal. The Holy Spirit used the verses below to make me stronger and find victory over my sickness.

Deuteronomy 31.6: *"...Be strong and courageous. Do not fear or be in dread of them, for it is the Lord your God who goes with you. He will not leave you or forsake you."*

Psalms 138.3: *"On the day I called, you answered me; my strength of soul you increased."*

Proverbs 3.5-6: *"Trust in the LORD with all your heart, and do not lean on your own understanding. In all your ways acknowledge him, and he will make straight your paths."*

Matthew 11.28-29: *"Come to me, all who labor and are heavy laden, and I will give you rest. Take my yoke upon you, and learn from me, for I am gentle and lowly in heart, and you will find rest for your souls."*

2Corinthians 1.3-4: *"Blessed be the God and Father of our Lord Jesus Christ, the Father of mercies and God of all comfort, who comforts us in all our affliction, so that we may be able to comfort those who are in any affliction, with the comfort with which we ourselves are comforted by God."*

Psalms 18.6: *"In my distress I called upon the Lord; to my God I cried for help. From his temple he heard my voice, and my cry to him reached his ears."*

Psalms 33.20-22: *"Our soul waits for the LORD; he is our help and our shield. For our heart is glad in him, because we trust in his holy name. Let your steadfast love, O LORD, be upon us, even as we hope in you."*

Philippians 4.6-7: *"...do not be anxious about anything, but in everything by prayer and supplication with thanksgiving let your requests be made known to God. And the peace of God, which surpasses all understanding, will guard your hearts and your minds in Christ Jesus."*

1Peter 5.6-7: *"Humble yourselves, therefore, under the mighty hand of God so that at the proper time he may exalt you, casting all your anxieties on him, because he cares for you."*

Ecclesiastes 3.1: *"For everything there is a season, and a time for every matter under heaven."*

John 14.1-3: *"Let not your hearts be troubled. Believe in God; believe also in me. In my Father's house are many rooms. If it were not so, would I have told you that I go to prepare a place for you? And if I go and* *prepare a place for you, I will come again and will take you to myself, that where I am you may be also..."*

Romans 8.16-17: *"The Spirit himself bears witness with our spirit that we are children of God, and if children, then heirs — heirs of God and fellow heirs with Christ, provided we suffer with him in order that we may also be glorified with him."*

Romans 8.24-25: *"For in this hope we were saved. Now hope that is seen is not hope. For who hopes for what he sees? But if we hope for what we do not see, we wait for it with patience."*

Romans 8.38-39: *"For I am sure that neither death nor life, nor angels nor rulers, nor things present nor things to come, nor powers, nor height nor depth, nor anything else in all creation, will be able to separate us from the love of God in Christ Jesus our Lord."*

1Peter 1.3: *"Blessed be the God and Father of our Lord Jesus Christ! According to his great mercy, he has caused us to be born again to a living hope through the resurrection of Jesus Christ from the dead."*

You can do the same. Don't look at your circumstances. Keep your eyes on the One who can give you victory over your circumstances.

8

Timeline

"I consider that our
present sufferings are not worth
comparing with the glory that
will be revealed in us."
- Romans 8:18

When I look back and see the healing journey
I went through, only one thing comes to mind:

"I waited patiently for the Lord;
he turned to me and heard my
cry. He lifted me out of the
slimy pit, out of the mud and
mire;he set my feet on a rock
and gave me a firm place to
stand. He put a new song in my
mouth, a hymn of praise to our
God. Many will see and fear the
Lord and put their trust in him.
Blessed is the one who trusts in
the Lord"
- Psalm 40:1-4

- 2010 — Found lump

- 09/2/2011 — Lumpectomy

- 10/04/2011 — Test results positive for cancer

- 11/14/2011 — Double mastectomy with reconstruction

- 12/12/2011 — Port placement

- 12/13/2011 — 1st chemotherapy

- 12/27/2011 — 2nd chemotherapy

- 01/10/2012 — 3rd chemotherapy

- 01/24/2012 — 4th chemotherapy

- 02/07/2012 — 5th chemotherapy

- 02/20/2012 — 6th chemotherapy

- 02/22/2012 — Trip to China

- 03/06/2012 — 7th chemotherapy

- 03/20/2012 — 8th chemotherapy

- 06/22/2012 — 2nd part of the reconstruction and port removed

9

Clear Eyes

"Then the Lord replied:
'Write down the revelation and
make it plain on tables so, that
a herald may run with it.'"
- Habakkuk 2:2

In October, 2011, my youngest daughter was
17 years old. At that time we received the test
results. She was already going to University
of Central Florida but she was still living at
home. I can't image what was going through
her head. But when she showed me what she
wrote I praised the Lord. She got it!! The Holy

Spirit gave her clear eyes to see Jesus's victory over cancer.

"Tears of Sorrow, Tears of Joy"

Tears well up in hopeless agony.

My own mother stricken by a mighty infirmity.

I see the disease through my human eyes.

Cancer, a raging villain, a destroyer of lives.

My family, my world its latest victim.

But my God, my Redeemer challenges the system.

As the scales fall, I see cancer in a new light.

Puny and frail compared to my Savior's might.

For "surely He took up infirmities and carried our sorrows" Isaiah 53.4

Isaiah unknowingly acknowledged my insecurities.

But Christ knowingly took up that infirmity.

So now with clear eyes and a hopeful heart I see cancer only as a playing part.

In God's immense plan for us.

So all is left to do is to let go, and trust.

For its in the hands of the all knowing King.

And with arms raised, lips pray and sing.

For victory in Christ Jesus, the Lord will bring!

By Gabriela Carmo

10

Prayer

"Hear my cry, O God, listen
to my prayer."
- Psalm 61:1

If you're going through a time of your life where you received bad news, please take the first step to trust God.

Yes you and I are not perfect. We make mistakes all the time that keep us away from our Heavenly Father. But Jesus Christ paid for all our mistakes. We just need to accept his sacrifice for us.

He is preparing a place for us so we can spend eternity with Him.

If you want to receive His gift for you and me, just pray this simple prayer:

Jesus I know I have made mistakes.

But I accept your payment for my sins.

I believe You died for them but You're now alive.

I want one day to live with you in Heaven.

Please help me to go through life with hope of my eternal future with You.

After you pray this prayer reach out for someone who has made the same decision you just did. You're part of God's family and you will never be alone!

You can send me an e-mail too if you want to share this experience with me too.

Thank you for be willing to hear about my journey!

I want you to know that I'm praying for you!

I hope my experience can be an encouragement to you and anyone going through a rough time.

You didn't get this book by mistake. I believe the Lord placed it in your hand and He can change your history if you let Him.

Please feel free to contact me to share your journey with me.

carmemcarmo@hotmail.com

"May God the Father and our Lord Jesus Christ give you grace and peace. Jesus gave his life for our sins, just as God our Father planned, in order to rescue us from this evil world in which we live. All glory to God forever and ever! Amen."
– Galatians 1:3-5

81233199R00028

Made in the USA
Columbia, SC
26 November 2017